Screams Of Love

When it just gets too heavy to carry all the
pain that the love caused ..!!

Avani sejwal [Tulip]

Made with ❤ on the BookLeaf Publishing Platform
www.bookleafpub.in
www.bookleafpub.com

Dedication

*For the one sided lovers who suffer alone. And
For the ones who aren't bothered about them!!*

Preface

So I am writing this book to let today's generation know how much pain love cause. Someone once told me that love can only give you pain. I didn't believe that person but now I am too forced to use the same words love can only give us pain. That's true. So please I suggest you guys that if somebody is ready to do anything for you never offend them. It hurts. It hurts alot.

Acknowledgements

So first of all very thanks to my parents who supported me the best to actually get my book published. Thanks to God who set a thought in my mind to be a writer. Thanks to my friends who always motivated me and appreciated my deep written poetries and thoughts.
And at last
A thanks to myself..that I never gave up even when sometimes I wasn't appreciated even when I wanted to give up but I never did. And thanks to those people who said that becoming a writer isn't for you. Now I will be proving them that it was always meant for me.
Thanks to you too the readers for making time to read my book..!!♡ ♡

1. We had a moment

Ever saw heaven on earth,
Or beautiful flowers in autumn?
I never believed on magic before.
Until we had a moment together.

Beautiful characters, mesmerizing novel.
Fictional love , truthful confessions.
I never believed in love before.
Until we had a moment together.

Can you just teleport here?
It was just a coincidental encounter of ours.
I never wanted someone.
Until we had a moment and I dreamt of forever

Sun can give pain,
Lightening can provide comfort.
Even if you put me through hell .
I would still feel blessed of that moment when I first saw

you as heaven.

2. If I could..! ♡

Sparkling stars and unreached heights ,
Comfy bed and noisy lights.
Walking with you near the tides..
A dream if I could turn real a million times.
Rabbits over the moon , mermaids in the ocean.
Astronauts in the sky and fishers beneath the sea.
Difference between real and imaginary...
If I could just swap up these.
Followed promises and lies unsaid,
Promises broken and truths hidden
I wish you could see that I promised and never lied.
And if you could just do the same for me ..then in love I
would've never died..!! ♡ ♡

3. I'm in love ..!♡

Rain sounds like music.

Hell feels like heaven.

Lies sound sweet.

Truths are hidden.

Seems like when I wake up birds chirp out your name.

You're my only wish when it's 11:11 everyday.

My only reason of being happy is you.

And for crying too.

Time can stop.

Posion can give life.

Violins can sound dumb.

Eyes can lie.

My every line describes you when I go on writing.

I'll only pray when I've a blessing for you in my eyes.

I sing those love songs very deeply like you're listening.

But you really doesn't.

Unsaid words.

Twisted lies.

Tearful eyes.

Fake smile.

I am in love but baby..
It's only from my side..!!♡♡

4. Unsaid

My eyes waiting for yours to look into mine.
Many words are left unsaid inside my mouth.
Unsaid wishes , Unsaid promises
Unsaid blessings and Unsaid truths too.
I am bad with words and you're bad in reading eyes.
Unsaid feelings , Unsaid love
Unsaid prayers and Unsaid words
Baby I held an eye contact everytime but I am bad with
words and you are bad in reading eyes..!♡

5. I wish you knew...

How easy is it to say that I don't care but
I wish you knew how my friends saw me crying in your
absence, I was feeling stupid to love you.
Yes you think that I don't like you ...I never really replied
back face to face when you said " I love you." But
I wish you knew how I was sleeping peacefully but felt
awake at 3 AM thinking of you.
You can think and you may believe that I still didn't get
over from my first love but..
I wish you knew that you took my heart way too easily
than he ever could.
I may say to you that I dream of you very rarely but
I wish you knew that you were the thought of mine
when people everytime caught me daydreamin' even in
the night too.
I said to many that if you left me I can still live but I wish
you knew that I would never feel happy if you left like
the way I was with you..
I may laugh..
I may smile

I may act alive too but if you left
I would no longer be able to feel me and I wish for you
to know this all before it may happen too..!♡

6. Hate me..

Hate me so much that if I die tomorrow the word coming
out from your mouth be " Luckily "

Darling hate me the more you can but
I'll still love you more than that
One day you'd ask yourself why you hate me this much
but I still loved you much than that..
It's okayy even if my love was one sided ,
I never really wanted to pressurize you...
Maybe you were meant to hate me and
I was meant to love you..! ♡

7. It feels like...! ♡

It's been a few days since I didn't see you..
It feels like January is turning into December..
I am feeling way too blue
it feels like my heart is attached with me by a glue.
My writing feels dumb because
My heart is way too numb.
Attachment is scary you know..
It feels like my heart isn't beating anymore..
Cause all it felt like was
I smiled because of you..
I cried for you..
And I denied my mind's choice when it said I should die
too..
it feels like you know how I am feeling and I can also tell
you what you'll ask a million times
I can no longer smile no longer cry...
It feels like I haven't met you since ages and it's useless
to bring up such things infront of people twice..
Yes you're not here

You can no longer hear me but..
It would feel like home when again we will meet.!♡

8. I don't want to..

I don't want to think , if the thoughts aren't you..
I don't want to speak if the words aren't you..
I don't want to see , if the view isn't you...
I don't want to be a poet , if the poetry isn't you..
I don't want to capture if the moment isn't you..
I don't want to pray if my wish isn't you..
I don't want to live , if the reason isn't you..
I don't want to die if even after dying I can't have you..!!
♡♡

9. I don't know...

I may give my life hundred times for you..
If you'll ask me to drink poison...
I will drink it too..
But I don't know if you will do the same for me...
Will you??

I want to beg you so that you don't leave...
If you'll ask I'll also be on my knees..
And tell you please stay...
But I don't know if you'll do the same for me..!!♡

10. If you are...! ♡

If you are my morning , I would love to wake up.
If you are my way , I would love to walk..
If you are sunset , I would love to watch you.
If you are bad , I would love to have you as my luck.
If you are a thought, I would love to think.
If you are tears , i would love to make a river flow from
my eyes.
If you are pain , I would love to be hurted.
If you are addiction , I would love to get ruined.
If you are a dream , I would love to sleep.
If you're a graveyard, I would love to be a dead body.
If you are a demon , I would love to be hypnotized.
If you are a jail , then I would love to be prisoned.
If you are ocean , I would love to drown.
If you are my fear , I would love to never overcome it.
If you are a cure , I would love to have a disease.
If you are a disease , I would love to never get over you.
If you are my life , I would love to live and
If you would've been death I would've definitely died
earlier...! ♡

11. Him..! 

If I cried , the tears would be him.
If I smiled , that smile would be him.
If I am hurted , the pain would be him.
If I am wet , then the rain would be him.
If I am freezed , then the time would be him.
If I am shining, my brightness would be him.
If I am asleep , my dream would be him.
If I am the poet , then the poetry would be him.
If I am living, then the reason would be him and..
If I died, the death would be definitely him..!♡

12. Strangers again! ♡

It was raining in midnight
I got up and wrote some lines
And when I turned the pages backward I realized
That we're strangers again in a very short time.

I still cry myself to sleep
hoping for you to come hug me and say
" Let's start it all over again " but then a flashback
that we were not meant to be in this lifetime.

I dream of you when I sleep and I dream of you
even when I am awake.
How sad that we are words of a stupid poem now.
As we're strangers again.

I feel your hands over mine when it's freezing cold.
As you are still there to warm me up like before.

But as we're strangers again
I can't think of more.!!♡ ♡

13. Failed..

My hands failed to see that his hands would never hold
mine.
My legs failed to see that his steps will never come
across mine.
My dreams failed to see that his dreams would never
wish me.
My luck failed to see that his days were going bad
because of me.
My eyes failed to see that he wasn't the one I deserved..
At last my destiny failed to see that we were just not
meant to be!!♡♡

14. You may...! ♡

You may be happiness in someone's life and sadness in others.

You may be good luck in someone's life and bad luck in others.

You may be the star in someone's life and moon in other's.

You may be the reason to live in someone's life and the reason to die in other's.

But if you're loved by me...

You'll be my everything which my eyes shouted but my mouth didn't even utter!! ♡ ♡

15. What should I do..!?

What should I do?!♡

If I woke up , I only think about him.

If I sleep , then I start to dream about him.

If I write , my everyline perfectly suits him.

If I dance , my each step would be craved for him.

If I sing , my feelings in that song would be for him.

If I am living then the reason would be him.

If I died then this sacrifice of mine would be dedicated to him!♡

16. Incomplete love...

Why did I meet you?
To make my heart shattered?
Or was that a coincidence?
Of our ways crossing eachother.

I never really wrote poetry, but now I do
Is it because of you?
The one who write poetry with graves..
Are poets who do have a heart but only glued.

Oops ! I forgot I never really had a heart..
It was with you the whole time.
But you realized you had only one..
Mine you drowned into the ocean of trying million
times..

I wanted to hate you like I would be able to say..
" I hope you die "
but you are the reason I am living for...
How can I lose you infront of my eyes?!♡

17. Are we gonna be alright?!

Hurtful jokes , stupid lies.
That's what our flirty lines and truths turned like...
Fake promises saying forever
Are we gonna be alright?
I'm doubting every inch of ours
Every moment that turned into a memory.
Cursing eachother and hating eyes..
Are we gonna be alright?!♡

18. Wake me up!!♡

It was you and I at first
But it all changed.
Wake me up baby
I don't feel like dreaming anymore.
Nightmares would feel good with you
If you can't be in a good dream of mine.
Wake me up baby...
Circumstances changed the time.
I would've kept you safe after wholly getting you.
But i didn't even had you a little...
I wish to wake up from my imaginations now..
Cuz you provided me love so bitter!!♡

19. I can't...

Ever since our ways drifted apart...
I can't feel anything else other than scars over my heart.
You can move on and you can forget..

But baby I can't.

Deep pain inside my heart ,

There's no light left

You can smile and laugh again...

But even if I feel like laughing again I can't.

You will always be in my heart locked..

Cuz I displaced it's key..

You can give your heart to someone else...

But no one will ever take your place in my heart♡

20. Sometimes...

There's a person in my life who I love to see everyday
and sometimes
I doesn't like him to see at all.
Sometimes I crave so hard to talk to him and
Sometimes silence is the only thing that
I expect between us.
Sometimes I become afraid thinking that we'll never
meet again...
And sometimes I become afraid thinking that
I will have to face him again.
Sometimes I feel like wishing so that I don't feel such
type of pain again...
But sometimes after seeing him I feel like falling in love
like this again!!♡♡

21. Ever since you left...! ♡

I feel like I am drown in your memories.
I feel like I am just lost in your thoughts...
I feel like I am meant to keep you in my prayers..
I feel like this way ever since you left , not from my
life...but you also left as a person who was once a
comfort zone for me. We used to be excited to talk with
eachother.
But it all changed ever since you left.
My love , I'm still here waiting for you to grow a garden
in my heart where only storms are taking place ever
since you left..! ♡